The Tapestry of Emotions

ROOHI BHARGAVA

BLUEROSE PUBLISHERS
India | U.K.

Copyright © Roohi Bhargava 2024

All rights reserved by author. No part of this publication may be reproduced, stored in a retrieval system or transmitted in any form or by any means, electronic, mechanical, photocopying, recording or otherwise, without the prior permission of the author. Although every precaution has been taken to verify the accuracy of the information contained herein, the publisher assumes no responsibility for any errors or omissions. No liability is assumed for damages that may result from the use of information contained within.

BlueRose Publishers takes no responsibility for any damages, losses, or liabilities that may arise from the use or misuse of the information, products, or services provided in this publication.

For permissions requests or inquiries regarding this publication, please contact:

BLUEROSE PUBLISHERS
www.BlueRoseONE.com
info@bluerosepublishers.com
+91 8882 898 898
+4407342408967

ISBN: 978-93-6452-961-7

Cover Design: Sadhna Kumari
Typesetting: Pooja Sharma

First Edition: August 2024

Dedication

To my readers
To everyone who has a story to tell to the world.

Preface

The Tapestry of Emotions, *the book, compiles heartfelt poetry intricately weaving threads of human emotions into a rich tapestry. Its themes span a range of human experiences, from love, distress, and pain to raw emotions and more, all intertwined with our daily realities.*

I am thankful to the Divine for another chance to prove myself. My deepest gratitude goes to my parents, family, and friends for their steadfast belief in me. Lastly, I extend thanks to my publishers, the Bluerose team, for their trust and support in bringing this beautiful book to fruition.

*With great pride, I present **The Tapestry of Emotions** to the world. I hope readers discover relatable stories within its pages. Thank you to everyone who takes the time to read it.*

Contents

Dedication *1*

Preface *3*

Love in Spring *1*

Season of Love *2*

Our Shared Dreams *3*

My Soulful Dream *4*

The Allure of True Love *5*

Gazing into Love *6*

Unconditional Love *7*

Through the eyes of love *8*

Holding on to Us *9*

Curating Love *10*

Fragrance of Love *11*

Heartfelt Imprint *12*

Wishing on You *13*

Harmony of Love *14*

Love's Perfect Brew *15*

The coffee date *16*

Pretentious Love *17*

My Sauve Love *18*

Ache in Ardor *20*

Love's Symphony *21*

Shattered Essence of Love 23

The Maze of Love 24

Love's Echoing Memories 25

Rekindling Love 27

A sweet Soul 29

A Soul's Life 30

Peace for the Soul 31

The Creator's Daydream 32

Perfectly Imperfect Soul 33

Lonely, Strange Soul 34

Unloving the Soul 35

Caged Soul 36

Fragile Facade 37

True Essence 38

If Only …. A Happy Soul 39

Healing Rain 40

The Silent Doll 41

The Magical Princess 42

A New Soul 43

A Story of Solitude 44

The Mellow Heart 45

Her True Essence 46

The Transformation Within 49

Ocean of Emotions 50

Tangled Emotions 51

Her Remembrance	*52*
Veiled Emotions	*53*
Charade of Affection	*54*
The Emotional Palette	*55*
Essence Unveiled	*56*
Unvoiced Emotions	*57*
Joy of Missing Out	*58*
Melancholy Musings	*59*
Shadows of Melancholy	*60*
Heart's Ascent	*61*
Scented Serenity	*62*
The Essence of Acceptance	*63*
Echoes of the Deep	*64*
Unraveling Emotions: From Homey to Stranger	*65*
Whispers of Resilience	*66*
Melancholy Vibes	*67*
Unloving the Soul	*69*
Come Back Soon	*70*
Rewind the tape	*71*
Forgotten Corners	*72*
An old photograph	*73*
Heaven's Symphony	*74*
Let's become strangers again!	*75*
Seized, Yet Loved!	*76*
Broken Ties	*77*

The Tapestry of Emotions'

Unloving: A Hard Journey	78
The Illusion of Paradise	80
Fragments of Heartache	82
Essence in Flight	85
The Challenging Life	86
Vision of Life	87
Life Crisis	88
Life's Dreams	89
Autumn Heals	90
The Life	91
Chaos and Life	92
An Ode to Life	93
Beyond the Limits	94
Tranquility of Life	95
Heartfelt Realities	96
Two Sides of Life	97
Embracing Life	98
A Fresh Canvas	99
Essence of Life	100
Let it Be, It's Life!	101
Melancholy Vibes	102
Summer Love	105
Nature's Symphony	106
A New Start	107
The Ticked Messages	108

Beyond the Breaking Point *109*
Real Connections *110*
The Healing Beats *111*
Open Letter to AI *112*
Tests of patience *113*
Love's Mending Touch *114*
Ode to Water *115*
Limited Edition *116*
The Unopened Heart *117*
Goodbye *118*
Second hand *119*
Third party *120*
If only *121*
A simple wish *122*
A Mishap of Feelings *123*
Healing through your love *124*
Seeking Light *125*
Unseen Generosity *126*
The Real Thing *127*
The Midpoint of Us *128*
Too Near, Too Far *129*
Don't go *130*
Together But Quite *131*
The Solitude We Choose *132*
Socially Compatible *133*

The Tapestry of Emotions'

Skin	*134*
Erasing you	*135*
Close Friends	*136*
Forbidden Love	*137*
Lack of Routine	*138*
Everyday	*139*
Coming to an end	*140*
Veiled Sentiments	*141*
At last	*142*
Kite of Dreams	*143*
The Hardest Goodbye	*144*
Falling Leaves, Rising Hope	*145*
Hope of Love in the Dark	*146*
Road to redemption	*147*
Unwritten Emotions	*148*
Societal Irony	*149*
A Soul's Aspiration	*150*
Abstruse Reality	*151*
The Sailor Saga	*152*
A Tapestry of Trust	*153*
A New Bud	*154*
Let it Be	*155*
Absence of Longing	*156*
Whispers to the Divine	*157*
Sacred Reflections	*158*

Story of Home *159*
Solitary Murmurs *160*
Etched in Memory *161*
The Dice of Destiny *162*
The Unseen Struggles *163*
Chords of Calm *164*
Why? *165*
About the Author *166*

The Tapestry of Emotions'

Love in Spring

*waiting
for roses to bloom
in the amusing spring
life springing up with joy and love
spreading the fragrant[1] love
amidst the roses
& blooming.*

---

[1] *Pleasant or sweet smell*

Season of Love

its spring
a festival
buds blooming to flowers
colourful butterflies adorn[2]
birds chirping happy songs
it's the season of love.

---

[2] *Decorate*

The Tapestry of Emotions'

Our Shared Dreams

We dreamt of love
a place beneath the clouds
just you & me
& our dream of love.

My Soulful Dream

Thinking of you brings peace to my mind; solace[3] to my heart,
you're the morning dew that appears in my dreams
my present doesn't hold any space; you exist in my dreams.

---

[3] *Comfort in times of grief or discomfort*

The Allure of True Love

Love isn't always about kisses and fluff
a beautiful blessing; but called unlawful
It's not a game but an emotional idea
It's a feeling; appealing[4] and warm
Love is alluring[5] when it's true.

---

[4] *Attractive or pleasing*
[5] *Beautiful*

Gazing Into Love

amidst the floral valley
peering into eyes
close proximity[6]
lip-synced; a kiss of love.

---

[6] *Nearness in time, place and relationship*

Unconditional Love

*Broken yet charming, it's the soul
unconditional love, care
that's all the affection
one can spread around
inhaling worth
the soul takes
only
Love.*

Through the Eyes of Love

Your eyes are like postcards
they hold messages
for your loved ones
all from heart and soul
it's about love
the messages of the heart
sent through the eyes.

Holding on to Us

Sadness rings in when we're apart
distraught[7] feeling of loneliness bugs me;
when you're away
I am left alone;
when you're away
and I pray for you to come back to me and hold me
let's relive our love again
just the two of us.

---

[7] Worried, nervous or upset

Curating Love

curating a character
her juncture[8]
filling with aspiration
living, dreamy entity[9]
piety[10]
she lives with all her passion.

---

[8] *A place where things join*
[9] *Something that exists*
[10] *Quality of being religious*

Fragrance of Love

Fragrance blooms in the air
Love is echoing in the sky
Oaths of flower-bloomed valley
Where the lovers' hearts find solace
Edged by roses, tulips and lilies
Radiating the fragrance of love
Settling into the beauty of true love.

Heartfelt Imprint

Your memories are etched on the memory card of my heart,
Yeah, we're far away
Yet our hearts entwined[11].
You're unable to accept,
But it's the truth.
Firsts always stay, etched[12] not only in minds but hearts
And you're the first,
I've loved with my soul.

---

[11] *Twisted together*
[12] *Defined*

Wishing on You

*A simple wish
To hold you close
To believe that you love me
And to feel the love
As you entwine your hand with mine,
It's simple; I just want to fall in love with you.*

The Tapestry of Emotions'

Harmony of Love

---

be the soul whom people love
hold care and love
be the rock to rely on,
so that the love can multiply,
be the home to the broken souls.
show love and care, and nourish all the folds,
spread harmony, and secure the bliss of a harmonious[13] love.

---

[13] *Tuneful*

Love's Perfect Brew

Love is like a tea for two
brews in the pot of life
a lot of love and a little bitterness
warm hugs and some harsh words
a lot of talks of the town
that's how they brew the love
all in friendship brew.

The Coffee Date

A lot of things can happen,
over a cup of coffee; only if you muse[14],
a trail of thought could make a soulful conversation,
as the coffee melts into your soul.
It's hard to stay away,
with caffeine taking a toll,
and you end up sharing feelings,
that you held in your heart,
of all that blissful love that we always share.

---

[14] Source of inspiration

Pretentious Love

She's amused by amour[15],
He killed her with desire.
His amour amused her,
His desire vanquished[16] her.

---

[15] *love*
[16] *defeat*

My Sauve Love

I am a naive soul,
Life's harsh and arduous[17],
Holding, a task endlessly,
I think and move over the thorny trail,
To find my safe haven, on the endless, lone tail
I found you in the alley,
Handsome, Chic and Sauve[18], a New You
It's urbane[19] you
And your rich aura
I fell in love
giving my heart to you
for, you'll handle me with your mature love.

Falling in love with you,
alluring and graceful,
You're suave and peaceful
I found love in your eyes and home in you
beautiful smile, chuckles, and laughter, yeah, that's you
You instilled love in me
Made me believe power of love
your gentle love

---

[17] difficult
[18] Charming, elegant
[19] Cultured; Sophisticated

It's all about you
I fell in love
giving my heart to you
for, you'll handle me with your mature love.

Ache in Ardor

I'm falling out of love,
With all the ugly scars,
You've pierced my soul and heart,
By unloving actions,
You've broken my palate[20].

I'm falling out of love,
You've pulled away from love,
Promise of forever,
You forgot love moments,
Crushing love for ever.

I'm falling out of love,
Our Love is vanishing,
You're no more the same,
Turned away from my soul,
Igniting a hurt flame.

I'm falling out of love,
Unloving is a pain,
Causing ache in ardor[21],
You're hurting me hard,
Falling out of amour.[22]

---

[20] *Preference*
[21] *Love*
[22] *Love*

Love's Symphony

With a simple essence[23],
I'm a flawed, sketchy[24] soul,
Drowned in intimacy,
Hoping you feel the same,
Immersed in ecstasy[25].

With a simple essence,
I expect love and care,
You're my sauve delight,
Handsome, chic gentleman,
You're my urbane sight.

With a simple essence,
I cherish your passion,
Pure love is alluring,
You're sweet and graceful.
You're true, enticing[26].

---

[23] Most significant element
[24] Not detailed
[25] A state of extreme happiness
[26] Attractive, tempting

With a simple essence,
I'm falling in your love,
You instilled love in me,
It's all about us, ours,
As you deeply love me.

The Tapestry of Emotions'

Shattered Essence of Love

Love is a bewitching[27] passion
can't be measured in contention[28]
causing oppressive affliction[29].

Loving with emotion and essence is appealing
but losing your intellect[30] to someone is degrading
for, you see your priority & harmony decreasing.

You've pierced my sole quintessence[31]
losing all my love's essence
led me to repent my choice.

Using me as toy
you have snatched my joy
your love, so phoney[32].

you broke love to bits
my heart into pieces
Ruined beyond repairs.

---

[27] *Powerfully attractive or charming*

[28] *arguments*

[29] *Cause of pain*

[30] *The power of reasoning and understanding*

[31] *Most significant element; synonym of essence*

[32] *Not genuine*

The Maze of Love

I'm one of a kind, lonely and deep,
You're another kind, lively and shallow,
I'm immersed in my passion,
You're busy making a vocation[33],
I've dropped what's disturbing,
You've opted for what's expected,
I am looking for peace,
You're mingling in the crowd,
We're two souls, beaut[34] of their kind,
I'm looking for love in myself,
You're seeking love out of yourself,
Life's nothing but a game,
Love's no less than a maze,
They sync together to make life full of love.

---

[33] career

[34] beautiful

Love's Echoing Memories

People will come & go, finding liberty,
Life is a bliss, changing every moment,
Our love will become a sweet memory.

You arrive in my heart, so gently warm,
Warming my heart with love, so pure and true.

You changed my life, embraced vivacity,[35]
You made me fall in love, embracing me,
Our love will become a sweet memory.

You've blended in my essence, fully.
Filling my memory with love.

With time, our love grew deep, beaut & classy,
I immersed myself in deep compassion,
Our love will become a sweet memory.

Blended with my soul, a peaceful whole,
You love me with passion.

You're a handsome, chic, sauve & loving guy,
Our love is beautifully carved, soulful,
Our love will become a sweet memory.

---

[35] Soul

Your love is pure and sauve,
drawing me to plumb the depths of your soul.

My eyes settle for nothing less than you,
You're my calm in the chaotic world, soon,
Our love will become a sweet memory.

You've defined love in a beautiful way,
Sharing unconditional love, & cheering
You've brought me passion, essence & empathy[36],
Our love will become a sweet memory.

---

[36] *Ability to understand emotions of other people*

The Tapestry of Emotions'

Rekindling Love

Love is beautiful when it's respected.
It's a dual effort to beautify the bond.
Binding all the love together,
Breaks if not cared for, loved, tended,
Setting the relationship to rest forever,

~begin to rekindle[37] the love~

Efforts come from within.
Revived with more love and affection,
It takes a second to break the affinity[38].
But a hundred efforts to rekindle,
It's all worth it when it's pure love,

~for love never ends, it stays~

Love stays in the vicinity[39] as long as you,
You've got to make amends[40], make alliances last longer,
There's no replacement for love,
and it always lasts for lifetime.

---

[37] *Revive*
[38] *Liking for someone*
[39] *Surroundings*
[40] *Make changes*

The Tapestry of Emotions'

A Sweet Soul

A soul
lonely, merry
she's an appealing fervour[41],
looking for magic, joy and love
yet spreading love and joy.

---

[41] Love

A Soul's Life

Born out of a shell,
I am a soulful essence[42],
Eager to gain acceptance,
Find passion towards life,
It's hard to intake essence,
and live life eloquently[43].

---

[42] Soul; most significant element

[43] Meaningful

Peace for the Soul

Peace is bliss and beaut,
Finding peace causes hurt,
You need to trust self,
And self-love is a truce[44],
The sole love for your soul.

---

[44] Agreement; interruption

The Creator's Daydream

She's a kind and funny girl and a creator,
Her name's April; she's silly to ponder[45],
Her funny acts and decorum[46]
lets her muse on the daydream[47]
when it breaks, letting her fall off her rocker[48].

---

[45] *To think about*
[46] *discipline*
[47] *A series of pleasant thoughts*
[48] *One's state of mind*

Perfectly Imperfect Soul

Water droplets on the parched[49] land
The rain drops down after a thunderstorm;
heaven cries, they say
rains cool down the weather;
and so does it to my heart,
my eyes cry the hidden emotions,
rain is perfect to hide those tears;
from those who are pretentious[50] and fake,
those who only break,
pure and sweet soul,
a broken heart,
rain-drenched, imperfect soul.

---

[49] *Very dry*
[50] *Importance; worth*

Lonely, Strange Soul

She's a lonely soul
Encompassed[51] by worries
Things turn around for her
Breaking her confidence in godly[52] presence
Pushing her into a strange pit
Pushing her into a stranger's shoes.

---

[51] surrounded.
[52] Religious

Unloving the Soul

I loved you with my whole heart, It's hard to unlove,
you came as a gentle breeze; but broke beyond fix,
I held you close to my heart, you crushed in pieces,
you have never loved me true, it's hard to unlove.

Caged Soul

Caged in life
Amidst insecurities
Chaotic[53] mess and aggrieved[54] soul,
that's a story of a lonely soul.

---

[53] *State of disorder*
[54] *Hurt; feeling resentment*

Fragile Facade

*Big little lies
can shake your presence,
for, life on lies in short-lived
if they can make you happy
they can break you too.*

True Essence

The real thing is,
Loving your own soul is true,
Being true to yourself,
Healing yourself with all the love,
is the real thing in the whole world.

If only .... A happy Soul

If only
I could say what's on my mind,
If I could tell the world how alone I am,
If only, I could share my pain and double my laughter with you,
If only.
I would have been a happy soul.

Healing Rain

grey sky; raining
raindrops tending[55]
healing the soul
the whole essence
stroll through life,
and healing the conscience[56].

---

[55] *Behave in a particular way*
[56] *Moral sense*

The Silent Doll

Life is hard, full of obstacles,
I am a doll of emotions,
Where people use as they please,
I stay silent, holding an eruption[57] of feelings, coz there is no one to listen,
It's the reality; being lonely in the world,
Be your own company; hold love for yourself,
And you'd not need anyone else to share outbreak your emotions.

---

[57] outbreak

The Magical Princess

She's the Queen of the Magicland,
weaving the magic spell of delight[58],
she dances away the sorrows in her dreamland,
she is the angel that everyone desire,
she relishes the taste of love in her wonderland,
wanting the dream-man to hug her,
to hold her close in his love-land,
she falls for him over again, holding him tight,
hey, she's the queen of her own enchanted[59] world.

---

[58] Great pleasure; joy
[59] Placed under a spell

A New Soul

she holds a sweet essence & deep emotion
she puts her family before her love
her love isn't wobbly[60]; full of devotion
she's lost in love; finding her treasure trove[61]
she finds joy in spreading sweet affection.

a gentle; timid soul; she's a princess
she finds solace in her distinct world
she tries to find words; and feelings to express
New beginnings, and her love and luck motioned.

---

[60] ending to move unsteadily from side to side.
[61] Collection of valuable or delightful things

A Story of Solitude

Spurring[62] on its own, that's love,
Seizing[63] my heart is your plan,
Taking hold of my soul and love,
Ripping[64] me for your own good; that's your love.

Wondering why you do that,
Holding all those grudges in heart,
Starting afresh is beautiful if you want,
Seizing my sanity[65], you're breaking my soul.

---

[62] *Urging*

[63] *A length of cord or rope*

[64] *Tearing*

[65] *The ability to think or behave in a certain manner*

The Mellow Heart

She's a mellow soul,
intertwined[66] with love,
holding mellifluous[67] hearts.
With chaotic surroundings,
full of mean environment,
she's turned mellow[68] to her life.
Amidst arduous[69] life,
she's become sober and mellow,
holding things in her heart,
setting an example for the planet.

---

[66] *Twisted or woven together*
[67] *pleasingly smooth and musical to hear.*
[68] *Soft or Gentle*
[69] *difficult*

Her True Essence

A sweet, peace-loving, joyous essence,
Searching for joy and happiness,
She's a lady of profound[70] grace.

An emotional intellect amidst chaos,
She is living her life, finding solace,
Holding quintessence[71] to make a truce with life.

An old soul, joyous with little things,
Finds amity[72] in this chaotic vivacity,
She's learning to unlove and live through it.

Unloving the world, loving the conscience[73],
It's her way to tackle hardships,
That's her true essence, her passion.

She's a lady of profound grace,
She holds on to love with zeal[74],
Believing in spreading love and delight.

---

[70] *deep*
[71] *Essence; core*
[72] *Friendly relations*
[73] *Self thought; moral sense of right or wrong*
[74] *energy*

The Tapestry of Emotions'

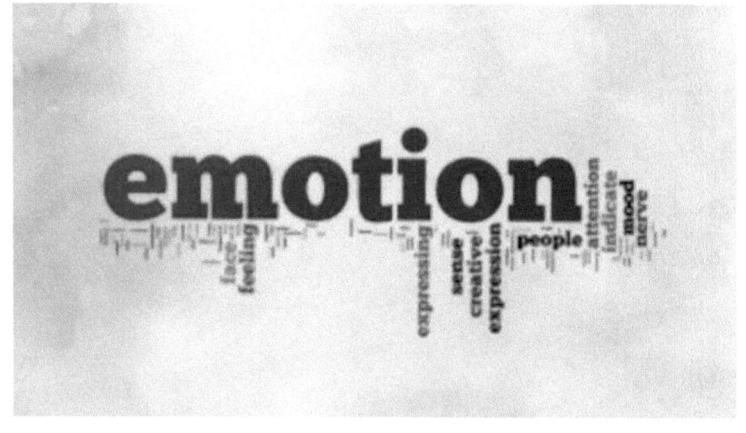

The Transformation Within

Holding emotions in her heart
Encompassing[75] the angst within her chest
She's turning into her strange self
Failing to trust the people
Demeanour[76] changing along
She's strange to her own soul.

---

[75] Hold within
[76] Outward behaviour

Ocean of Emotions

Emotions,
an ocean,
of pain & joy.

You may feel,
Hurt, crushed & mauled[77].
Yet smiling.

they take up,
key roles,
to shape soul.

---

[77] *wounded*

Tangled Emotions

My heart holds profound feelings,
It's throbbing[78], aggrieved[79],
Of all the chaos around,
Finding peace is packed,
Love is far immersed[80],
I'm looking for sanity,
Finding love, all bruised[81].

---

[78] Sound with a regular rhythm
[79] Unfairly treated
[80] Involved into something deeply
[81] hurt

Her Remembrance

---

*She was pretty and merry
a soul so kind and bubbly
she struggled and lived a life
worth remembrance for a whole life
she rests in deep sleep forever
her memories heart-etched ever.*

Veiled Emotions

Veiling[82] my emotions, I just fake-smile
None is understanding, assuming me to be happy,
But every smile holds pain
And every pain doesn't bring a smile to you,
I veil my inner turmoil[83]
To just move on in my life.

---

[82] Covering something

[83] A state of uncertainty, confusion

Charade of Affection

all emotional and enchanting[84]
believing in your soul so enthralling[85]
I fell in love with you
only to realize your shady self
becoming the fool in your fake love
a pawn[86] for the sake of love.

---

[84] *charming, delightful in a magical way*
[85] *Capturing and holding one's attention*
[86] *Being used*

The Emotional Palette

---

the place of emotions,
when the mind and heart entangle,
emotions take the backseat
& all that remains is practicality
everything hops on the backseat,
& what lies ahead is life

Essence Unveiled

*Garbage van
where you throw the emotions,
the agony and the guilt
you keep it in the heart
drowning in the beat
It's not the garbage van
for you to ruin your essence.*

Unvoiced Emotions

*A voice mail
sits unheard in the recorder,
his last message to her,
seeking apology for his deed,
she didn't give him a heed,
for, he left when she needed him,
and now, she's her own hero.*

The Tapestry of Emotions'

Joy of Missing Out

---

is beautiful,
when you love yourself,
follow simple pleasures,
and find joy.

Melancholy Musings

why is life rigid?
why are feelings so profound[87]?
why is distress[88] so sturdy[89]?

life is stiff & toilsome[90]
emotions are mistaken
and life is melancholy[91].

---

[87] *Deep*

[88] *Sorrow; pain*

[89] *Strongly built*

[90] *Involving difficult work; great work*

[91] *Sadness*

Shadows of Melancholy

why is it rigid?
why is life melancholy?
why it's distressful all through?

full of emotions
it's a beautiful essence
unknown, so melancholic[92].

---

[92] *Feeling sadness*

Heart's Ascent

soaring[93] in sky
let your emotions fly high
it's a kite.

a colourful palette
all of colourful, vibrant emotions
just fly high.

---

[93] *Flying high*

Scented Serenity

Roses, lilies, tulips
Blooming; fragrant

A field adorned with flowers
sweet haven on Earth.

The Essence of Acceptance

acceptance is the sweet essence[94]
you're the substance
love brings you bliss[95]
the soulful kiss.

when you worship your secret soul
life becomes whole
there's urgency
for ardency[96].

accepting your real soul self
loving oneself
the true essence
pure tenderness.

---

[94] *Most significant quality*
[95] *Perfect happiness; great joy*
[96] *enthusiastic*

Echoes of the Deep

Diving deep into the ocean of creativity; finding solace and peace
I find it hard to retain the composure and palace
I stare deep into darkness, fighting my concerns
Trying to find positivity in existence
Crying out my essence
Holding on
Life.

Assuring myself of a beautiful dawn, I decided to wait along
It is hard to walk on a bed of thorns
Getting closer to the destination also got deeper regrets
Staring deep into nothingness, I find
My soul, heart-breaking shiver
Taming self
soul

Unraveling Emotions: From Homey to Stranger

emotion

hidden and unspoken

holding feelings; all melancholy[97].

encompassing angst, sorrow and being moody

she turns dejected[98], tormented[99], mournful, & weary

homey turning into a drifter.

she changed her demeanor[100]

a stranger.

---

[97] *A feeling of sadness which lasts for a long time*
[98] *Sad or distressed*
[99] *Experiencing extreme physical or mental sufferings*
[100] *Outward behaviour*

Whispers of Resilience

She's a girl, pretty-pleasing
life is nothing less than daunting[101]
yet she's the one, always questioned
she lives a life so flawed, yet she's always smiling.

She's an angel in disguise[102]
her purpose of love & life complies
she's the family's true backbone
all alone, tied up with responsibilities

She often cries in her own realm
hiding her scars, she's overwhelmed
embraces the pain with bravery
a soul so waiver[103], she's deeply in love whelm[104]

She's a woman of love & essence,
she's always finding the responses
of all the "where", "why?" & all things soul
a being so whole, she, the knight[105] of her essence.

---

[101] *Difficult to deal*

[102] *Take a different appearance*

[103] *courageous*

[104] *Engulf; submerge*

[105] *someone born of the nobility and trained to fight*

Melancholy Vibes

Life is a melancholy vibe,
tracing through the dishevelled[106] path,
fighting for life with your own tribe,
and life makes you face its deep wrath.

Profound emotions make their space,
Feeling estranged[107] within a crowd,
Let chaos go & let life embrace,
Live your own life & make yourself proud.

Inner turmoil breaks tender heart,
Wander around limitlessly,
vague[108] sentiments break you apart,
and life's flowing relentlessly.

washes off the soul,
when people hurt, leave you alone
you're alone & life takes a toll,
and life takes exams out of zone.

The heart tangles with emotions,
yet, life is beaut & chaotic.

---

[106] *Untidy; disordered*
[107] *No longer close or affectionate to someone*
[108] *Unclear*

Unloving the Soul

I loved you with my whole heart, It's hard to unlove,
you came as a gentle breeze; but broke beyond fix,
I held you close to my heart, you crushed in pieces,
you have never loved me true, it's hard to unlove.

Come Back Soon

You've gone away too far,
I can't reach you, it's out of my power
Dear love, life is already hard
Do not make me deprived[109] of your love
Please, come back soon.

---

[109] *Suffering a severe lack of something*

Rewind the Tape

I want to go back and change a few stances[110],
Wishing for a rewind button, to change what's already done,
Rewind the tape,
Life could have been better.

---

[110] *the way in which someone stands*

Forgotten Corners

the moments that you drop
or those which lapse[111]
remain in your life
amidst your chaotic[112] soul,
they become the forgotten corners of your life.

---

[111] *Brief failure*
[112] *State of complete disorder*

An Old Photograph

being all the old memories.
when days were fun,
no secret kept
and only love remained,
sweet memories,
captured in photographs.

Heaven's Symphony

Water droplets on the parched[113] land
The rain drops down after a thunderstorm;
heaven cries, they say
rains cool down the weather;
and so does it to my heart,
my eyes cry the hidden emotions,
rain is perfect to hide those tears;
from those who are pretentious[114] and fake,
those who only break,
pure and sweet soul,
a broken heart,
rain-drenched, imperfect soul.

---

[113] *Dried out with heat*
[114] *Expressive of affected*

Let's Become Strangers Again!

*We came a long way
from strangers to friends
we connected through the soul,
bonding like sisters.
Fate had other plans,
we parted by the misunderstandings
things haven't been straight,
It's better, we become strangers again.*

Seized, Yet Loved!

Love is an emotion; spurring on its will,
it's not the same with you; you wanted to seize[115] my heart, my whole soul,
you didn't respect what I gave you,
you've just ripped me apart.
I'm wondering what makes you do so,
that you still hold grudges[116]; seizing my sanity,
with the unsaid and you're still free; flying beneath your own world.

---

[115] *To take hold of something suddenly*

[116] *a persistent feeling of ill will or resentment resulting from a past insult or injury.*

Broken Ties

Met by chance; we became sisters by soul, we've been open books to each other; constructing a harmonious bond, though things were found hidden beneath.

Time passed; the bond grew,
yet it broke; third person barged in,
opened books closed, the ties broke; for you inclined to them who praised the wrongs,
and the beaut story ended.

It's time to get along; if you like to start afresh,
re-construct the bond that we lived,
and let it flow until eternity.

Unloving: A Hard Journey

It's very easy to fall in love,
I fell for your gentle aura[117],
Why is it so hard to unlove?

You hold me in your embrace,
I feel the divinity of love,
It's very easy to fall in love.

You left me kaput[118] and broken,
I was alone; unable to let slip the love,
Why is it so hard to unlove?

On the alleyway when I found you,
I fell for your face; handsome, chic[119] and serene[120] smile,
It's very easy to fall in love.

You chose to play with me,
All the while I loved you; you took me for granted,
Why is it so hard to unlove?

---

[117] *A distinctive quality or character*
[118] *Broken and useless*
[119] *smart elegance and sophistication*
[120] *Calm, peaceful*

I didn't see it coming; fell deeply in love with you,
But you broke me into pieces; unmendable,
It's very easy to fall in love,
but why is it so hard to unlove?

The Illusion of Paradise

Life is passing by me,
Time is flowing at pace,
and I'm clueless, low pace,
Testing the patience and courage in me,
Leaving a broken heart & mistrusted[121] soul, that's me,
They start afresh with smile,
Faking the pain beneath the joy,
Treat me as toy,
Change colours in flash,
Take instant chance,
They flash a smile and enjoy,
The momentary joy of paradise[122].

Looking around my soul,
I find the distance from them,
Letting all the thoughts stream,
I'm left stunned at the harsh words for my soul,
Astonished at their thoughts, that's not my real soul,
Intaking all the pain,
I smile, holding them close to heart,
having soft spot,
nurturing with love,

---

[121] Be suspicious of

[122] An ideal state; heaven

Take instant chance,
Show them ire[123] and enjoy,
the reality of real paradise[124].

---

[123] Anger

[124] Heaven

Fragments of Heartache

She's a lone[125] soul,
Holding an essence,
Of profound love.

Her soul is grief-stricken,
For, she's dropped the chances,
That'd change her life.

Her life is messy,
She's trapped in a cage,
Fighting inner turmoil[126].

She's happy yet tangled,
In a chaotic race,
Between heart and mind.

A lot to say,
But she can't speak,
For, no one would understand.

She's turned solitary[127],
Immersed in her own world,
finding inner happiness.

---

[125] lonely

[126] a state of great disturbance, confusion, or uncertainty.

[127] Existing alone

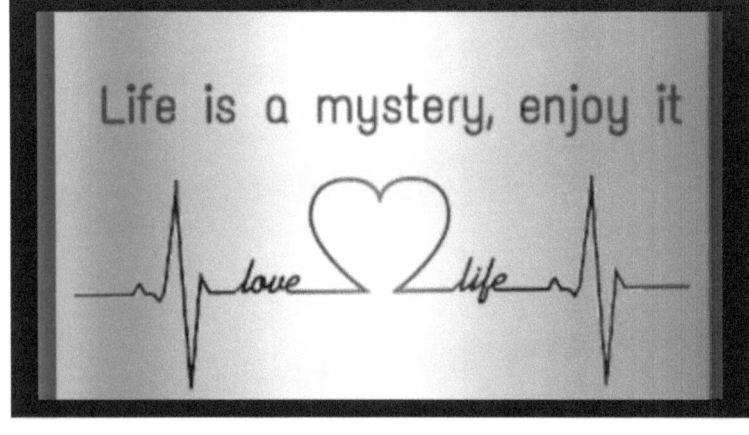

Essence in Flight

Might look easy, but life is hard,
Flying high, our zest[128] is rigid
We strive for essence,
on a hunter's use,
try to cross,
That's a Bird.

---

[128] enthusiasm

The Challenging Life

Pushing you outta[129] limits, life is challenging,
welcoming some fresh newness, banishing[130] the old,
that's the pretty rule of life, that's arduous[131] life,
hold it tight and love- nourish, banish hate; spread love.

---

[129] *Out of*
[130] *Getting rid of*
[131] *Difficult*

Vision of Life

Amidst the hill; under the trees
Savouring the morning breeze
I want to write my vision of love.
Those struggles and stories, I hold in my heart
I want to pen them down
Open my heart and tell the world
My vision of life.

Life Crisis

Life is at stake
Things haywire[132]
Luck in vain
Just a flow of unsurity
That's the crisis in life.

---

[132] *Out of order*

Life's Dreams

dreaming with open eyes & soul
my life; whole
reality dawns[133]; syncing
breaking dreams so magical
breaking trends; all mythical[134]
life trending.

---

[133] beginning
[134] fictious

The Tapestry of Emotions'

Autumn Heals

---

a sunny day
leaves gray, it falls
they play with wind
the kind sun heal
the mind awaits a life so real.

The Life

*Life is demanding; pushing you outta limitations,
bringing stress and dissatisfaction,
all of the frustration from life so twisted,
that's the game of life.
You'd be active and keep working,
imitating the conscious self; try holding a satisfying grin,
and resolve life problems; making life a happy zone.*

Chaos and Life

You, spirit,
chaos,
ways,
esprit[135].

Esprit's severe,
thick ends,
clutter
& fervor[136].

Fervor,
turmoil,
life-changing,
beautiful flexure[137]

Flexure,
change,
in chaos,
cher[138] You.

---

[135] life
[136] love
[137] turn
[138] pretty

An Ode to Life

I am grateful for this life, Oh God,
Life is hard,
Not easy to turn around or stop in the middle,
It's just a maze and it meddles
Every now and then with our lives,
Life is just a game.

Oh, Dear, life is a game of chances,
Play with mightiness[139],
be the winner.
Though not easy but you are a pawn,
In this esse[140] and be the dawn,
For your desire.

---

[139] *Quality of being powerful*
[140] *Existence; Actual Being*

Beyond the Limits

Life is challenging; pushing you outta limits,
welcoming some newness, banishing[141] the old,
that's the pretty rule of life.
Relations are like life; topsy-turvy,
they tend to break and fall,
just hold them right, nourish with love,
banish the hate and let love prevail.

---

[141] *Send someone away from a place or country*

Tranquility of Life

Life is chaotic,
moments are transient[142],
and distraught[143] environment,
it's the framework.
Chaos is disturbing for the soul,
yet tranquility[144] is difficult to find,
for the life is dramatic,
hurting the soul.
Tranquil[145] is a blessing,
when you fall in love with yourself.

---

[142] temporary
[143] Very worried and upset
[144] Peaceful, calm state
[145] Free from disturbance

Heartfelt Realities

Doing things with all your heart is beautiful,
dropping them without notice is hurtful,
not everything must be analyzed; especially those relations by heart,
they might be a frolic for you, but it's my love.
Life is all about analysing reality but not love,
for, it can neither be analyzed nor measured,
it might be lovers, family or friends, it's true when it's from the heart,
you can't name it frolic[146] and analyse every move,
for, it's the greatest blessing, if you realise,
otherwise, it's a game of analysis between heart and mind.

---

[146] *play or move about in a cheerful and lively way.*

Two Sides of Life

Two sides of a coin,
Lost and found are different,
Yet they are connected.
To the coin of life.

While finding your true self,
You lose a part of yourself.
Achieving what you wish for,
But you lose you heart.

That's the journey of lost and found,
Two sides of a coin, called life.

Embracing Life

accepting life with grace & delight
being the light
in the life maze
take life's deep gaze

life's harsh; it is all for real
love helps to heal
all emotion
healing passion
life is a game; live, love and play
worry at bay
challenging self
accept love; yourself.

A Fresh Canvas

starting afresh is a profound concept
holding grudges[147] in the soul is sorrowful
let go of the torment[148] that hurts your heart
the universe & nature is beautiful
letting you adopt the realm of concept

accepting the entirety of newness
dab the sorrow, accept the love and joy
experiment with your thoughtfulness
accepting new beginnings of true joy.

---

[147] *be resentfully unwilling to give or allow*
[148] *Severe physical and mental suffering*

Essence of Life

Life is a journey; it's full of surprises,
Every day is new where the soul rises,
Your dreams define your essence so churny[149],
It's full of surprises; life is a journey.

Emotions are beautiful; they reveal your soul,
They define the essence of the whole.
Emotional quintessence[150] is soulful,
They reveal your soul, emotions are beautiful.

Life is a canvas, you create your soulful art,
Art is nothing but it shows your intellect,
It's a journey of developing essence,
You create your soulful art, life is a canvas.

---

[149] To stir

[150] the most perfect or typical example of a quality or class.

Let it Be, It's Life!

the way you want it,
for, you don't want to change,
you're the victim and the rest world is attacker,
they pounce and you're whining,
that's your take to life,
that you're the only one who gets hurt.

Ever thought of those, whom you blame and hurt,
for, you're always right but, that can be wrong at times,
no one is so perfect,
but, let it be,
for, you won't realize ever.

Melancholy Vibes

Life is a melancholy vibe[151],
tracing through the dishevelled[152] path,
fighting for life with your own tribe,
and life makes you face its deep wrath.

Profound emotions make their space,
Feeling estranged[153] within a crowd,
Let chaos go & let life embrace,
Live your own life & make yourself proud.

Inner turmoil breaks tender[154] heart,
Wander around limitlessly,
vague sentiments break you apart,
and life's flowing relentlessly[155].

Ecstasy[156] washes off the soul,
when people hurt, leave you alone
you're alone & life takes a toll,
and life takes exams out of zone.

The heart tangles with emotions,
yet, the life is beaut & chaotic.

---

[151] *a distinctive feeling or quality capable of being sensed*
[152] *untidy*
[153] *No longer close/affectionate*
[154] *Showing gentleness, affection*
[155] *In a harsh way*
[156] *Overwhelming feelings*

The Tapestry of Emotions'

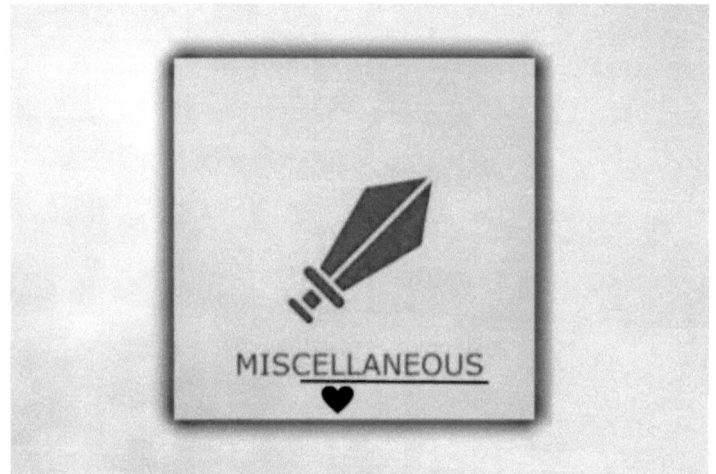

Summer Love

*Sun shining bright
Scorching heat and ice-cold water
Represent the summer, love.*

Nature's Symphony

Blooming rose
orange-hued sky
flight of birds
the cool breeze at night
pretty lights.
a cool gust of wind,
that's nature looker for the world.

A New Start

Beautiful morning
arises with upbeat
the sun's rays spread over
spreading bliss and delight

You've to shine lambent[157]
basking into fervour[158]
feeling peace and blissful
sharing the blithe[159] ardor[160].

---

[157] *Softly bright or radiant*
[158] *Intense and passionate feeling*
[159] *showing a casual and cheerful indifference*
[160] *Love*

The Ticked Messages

The blue ticks
They tell me how much you care for me
Blue ticks are the marks that make me realise that you're there for me
They're the only association left between us.

Beyond the Breaking Point

How to know it's a mistake
When everything seems falling apart
When trust seems broken
When the night's longer,
And the soul is sad
It's a mistake.

Real Connections

Less but real
My friends are fewer but real
They might not be clingy[161] but they are
They might not show but they love
They're real and the best of the lot.

---

[161] *Emotional dependant*

The Healing Beats

The playlist
The selected rhythmic beats
Holding the hem[162] of emotions
Calming the soul
They're the beats healing the voids.

---

[162] *The bottom edge*

Open Letter to AI

Take over what you're supposed to,
But do not take over the emotions
For, they're raw and no AI can hold them for long.

Tests of Patience

*Life tests
are happening every day
nothing is aligned in a way
life is happening, keeping joy at bay
it's hard to survive, in the chaos,
& patience is at edge,
testing every bit of life.*

Love's Mending Touch

How to fix a broken heart
Only love can heal,
The broken pieces of the heart,
Put the pieces of the soul back,
and that's how you can mend a broken heart.

Ode to Water

endure[163] *it,*
for, you savour it,
do not let it drop down your eyes,
for, it's the costliest,
holding unsaid emotions in a single drop.

---

[163] *suffer*

Limited Edition

When you find someone caring for you
When they think of you first
They're the limited edition
who love you more than they love their own soul.

The Unopened Heart

An unread message
Her uneven heartbeat
Waiting to be opened,
The soul to be read,
That too, through the gram.

The Tapestry of Emotions'

Goodbye

The toughest emotion
To wave goodbye
To part ways from love
And moving ahead
with a thousand scars.

The Tapestry of Emotions'

Second Hand

be a neat gift wrap,
letting people unwrap the best, in your face,
don't be a second hand,
for people to use and drop,
for life is enough to let you drop into difficult situations.

Third Party

It's about the emotion we hold,
all the mellow love,
and intertwined[164] hands,
why'd we need the third party,
to initiate conversation,
when we held our mellifluous[165] hearts altogether,
holding on to each other,
banishing the third person,
ogling[166] into our lives.

---

[164] *Twisted together*
[165] *Pleasingly smooth or musical to hear*
[166] *To stare at something*

If Only

I could say what's on my mind,
If I could tell the world how alone I am,
If only I could share my pain and double my laughter with you,
If only,
I'd been a happy soul.

The Tapestry of Emotions'

A Simple Wish

---

to hold you close,
to believe that you love me, and to feel the love as you entwine your hand with mine,
it's simple, that I just want to fall in love with you.

A Mishap of Feelings

Happened when I met you,
a clash of thoughts,
and a mishap[167] of feelings,
it happens because we've got different prospects,
yet we share all that's in heart,
coz it's a happy accident,
that we fell in love.

---

[167] An unfortunate incident

Healing Through Your Love

I was a mess and you held me close,
you made me realise that life is beautiful with the goodness,
and you held my pieces together and have me a new life,
It's just yesterday's happening, but you made me realise,
that friendship is beautiful,
being the base of True love.

Seeking Light

Walking through scorching[168] sunlight,
I run into the no man's Land,
amidst the darkness, I lose my way,
praying to the great Lord, tk pave my way.

---

[168] Very hot

Unseen Generosity

Nothing in the life is free of cost,
only the human has become thankless,
they need things at their comfort,
but they don't want to thank the power,
they're all mean,
and thankless to the universe,
which is the only reason of their existence.

The Real Thing

Loving your own soul is true,
being true to yourself,
healing yourself with all the love is the real thing in the whole world.

The Midpoint Of Us

*we've been in the middle of life,
thinking to either drop or continue,
with the ripped[169] bond we hold,
holding the two ends,
only to leave it in the midpoint.*

---

[169] *Badly torn*

Too Near, Too Far

I sit in the trance[170] that you'll come,
hold me in your embrace,
kiss my head with love, with your firm hands on my waist,
but hey, that's a daydream[171],
for you're too far sometimes, out of my hands,
and sometimes, you're too near, walking out of my hold,
our love is neither too far, nor too near.

---

[170] *State of mind*
[171] *a series of pleasant thoughts that distract one's attention from the present.*

Don't Go

Don't leave me alone,
Don't distance away,
for, you're the one I need,
Please don't go,
You're the only sunshine of my life, and the beat of my heart.

Together But Quite

We're together but not really,
you're quite far away, just in my dreams,
I can't have you in my reality,
for, it's difficult,
we're together in love, but not in the reality.

The Solitude We Choose

It's nothing but staying alone, away from a world that we choose,
Friendlessness is like being a parched[172] land,
Looking for path which is not in Vision.

---

[172] Very dry

Socially Compatible

I am asocial[173],
for, I love to stay alone,
read books and have the company of my thoughts,
I may not be socially compatible, but I surely a socialist, spreading positivity through my words.

---

[173] Not social

Skin

It's not my skin,
to be rude and arrogant,
it's not me if I thrash[174] you out,
it's not my skin to be the one I am not, neither my ethics allow me.

---

[174] *Beat repeatedly*

Erasing you

is the hardest thing to do,
I can't forget you,
for, you've been my calm,
I've loved you with all my heart and you're the only one to walk away,
But erasing you is the hardest thing to do.

Close Friends

Met as strangers,
Became close like sisters,
Connected by heart,
We chose to be the souls,
Who chose to fight the odds,
And rekindle[175] the love forever.

---

[175] To start again

Forbidden Love

I forbid you to enter my life,
for, you'd want me,
and I love you,
I might be a fantasy[176] to you,
but, for me, you're the beat of my heart,
but you chose to break me,
so, I forbid[177] your love,
without the permission.

---

[176] *Activity of imagining impossible*
[177] *Refuse*

Lack of Routine

---

makes life dull and boring,
but life keeps changing every now and then,
and a lack of routine may help you instill a routine and start afresh.

Everyday

Is a new day,
Full of new hopes and aspirations,
Everyday is beaut with love around,
And it becomes a new beginning.

Coming to an End

Every little thing comes to an end, be it life, love or friendship,
It's a relationship that stays with love,
it might be broken or torn,
coming to an end,
but can be felt with the instillation[178] of love.

---

[178] *a method used to put a liquid into the body slowly or drop by drop.*

The Tapestry of Emotions'

Veiled Sentiments

just like thoughts not shared,
some moments are better kept hidden,
some memories are better spent with love,
some poems are better not written, for they hold the heartiest feelings,
the poet doesn't want to share.

At Last

everything withers[179] with time,
what stays forever is the love that you hold,
memories made and life loved,
at the end, only the moments matter.

---

[179] Getting dry

Kite of Dreams

fly like kite
embrace your aspirations in heart
take a flight .

Live life freely
be the carefree, loving soul
fly like crate.

The Hardest Goodbye

---

leave

emotions

hollow space is left

creating a vaccum[180]

it's the hardest goodbye to your soul

---

[180] *a space absolutely devoid of matter*

Falling Leaves, Rising Hope

*Autumn
the leaves fall
making space for new
leafages, flowers and foliage
say goodbye; a new beginning.*

Hope of Love in the Dark

The hope of love stays forever,
Life is hardest game played ever,
emotions bubbling in the stare,
passion arises in the core,
sombre[181] yet enchanting, the emotion of love
where change is constant, there remains the hope of love.

In the dark, we lose the right way,
the stars are lighting the pathway,
with time, the flame could die, and leave
scars on soul, falling out of love
Love, enmity[182], ire[183], and sting[184]; all move in a lark[185],
falling out of love & hate, and living in the dark.

---

[181] *Dark or dull in colour or tone*
[182] *A state or feeling of opposition*
[183] *anger*
[184] *Wound with a sting*
[185] *Carefree adventure*

Road to Redemption

Life isn't a straight road,
you gotta walk, run or even jump,
you'll trip and fall, you'll be held a charge for toxicity[186],
Coz the society mentality is diseased.
You gotta shout and scream,
for, they'll never hear the meek voices,
you've to kill the toxicity,
And instil the emotion of love,
that'll cure the disease.

---

[186] *The quality of being toxic*

Unwritten Emotions

Emotions cause pain
Tries go in vain
You've turned stoic
And I am still static
Overwhelmed by your grimness[187]
You are still my weakness
I am overwhelmed [188]with my emotion
Where you still are in attraction
But I am just a blank page of your life.

---

[187] *The quality of being ugly or unpleasant*
[188] *have a strong emotional effect on.*

Societal Irony

Fearing "What will people say?"
Questioning "What do you do?"
and having no answers to them,
that's the societal fear.
Society dabs you, your passion,
questioning things that doesn't matter,
yet, stay still in what you do,
for, society will always blame,
what will only matter is fame.
That's the irony and that's what is society.

A Soul's Aspiration

Be an ambitious soul,
the one who strives to instil the self,
the soul you truly are,
you should hold the love, peace and solace,
and achieve your ambition.
You're innocent; you want to achieve the goals,
that's your ambition for life,
just to achieve it for yourself.

Abstruse Reality

Life is abstruse[189]; letting humans be the pawns,[190]
the puppets who play through others' fingers,
that is life in reality.

You may live in a fictional reality,
where there's nothing beyond love,
and life goes as per you,
but in reality, life goes as it pleases,
and you're just a pawn in the hands of the Great Lord.

---

[189] *Difficult to understand*

[190] *A person used by others*

The Sailor Saga

We're the sailor of our own boats,
the boat sails in the topsy-turvy life,
it turns the way we want, or it may sink,
so, keep on sailing, the boat of life.
It might be hard, but life's arduous,
it's not easy to swim across the vast ocean,
but life doesn't come with a manual,
you're the sailor and the writer of your destiny.

A Tapestry of Trust

We're close friends
Met by chance
Friends by choice
They opened their souls mutually.

They're strangers
One's shy, the other's assertive[191], diverse poles.
They got along, a friendship began,
Their hearts find solace[192] in one another.
A void is filled as they become close friends.

---

[191] Confident personality
[192] A person or thing that makes you feel happy

A New Bud

Newness is an opportunity,
a chance to renew the possibility,
turning the impossible into possible,
it's nothing but the faith to continue.

Every new beginning is an example,
a minute step can do wonders,
and if backed with brilliant ideas,
it may be hard,
but every new beginning is nice.

Let It Be

the way you want it,
for, you don't want to change,
you're the victim and the rest world is attacker,
they pounce and you're whining,
that's your take to life,
that you're the only one who gets hurt.

Ever thought of those, whom you blame and hurt,
for, you're always right but, that can be wrong at times,
no one is so perfect,
but, let it be,
for, you won't realise ever.

Absence of Longing

I feel the absence of longing,
in things I do; which are close to my heart,
the absence of longing is evident,
when there's no willingness,
and only pressure,
that's the real absence of longing. Don't leave me alone,
Don't distance away,
for, you're the one I need,
Please don't go,
You're the only sunshine of my life, and the beat of my heart.

Whispers to the Divine

---

you're the supreme lord
creator of this beautiful world
when my problems will be heard, I wonder.

wondering about the past
my anticipation for future
will I love my life, I wonder.

praying to my precious lord
my wishes being granted
will my prayers be answered, I wonder.

Sacred Reflections

---

reflect on your deeds
have faith in the supreme power
blessings will reflect on you, one good day.

life twirls at three-sixty degrees
love yourself rather than love
blessings will reflect on you, one good day.

reflect on the good memories,
the sorrows will come after,
blessings will reflect on you, one good day.

Story of Home

the heaven
love all around
beneath love
rebuke[193], find peace
the chaos
chaotic life
embrace the god's gift of home.

---

[193] Disapprove

Solitary Murmurs

the silence
speaks emotions
lone in crowd
beneath four walls
of a home
unfolding crux[194]
the reality of home

---

[194] A difficult problem

Etched in Memory

It's all gonna be a memory,
The life that we live will change.
People will come and go.
Only those who love you will stay,
Everything is temporary and so is life,
Live it to the fullest and make memories for a lifetime.

The Dice of Destiny

It's hard to live life
Without infecting the present
It's a game and dice connects the past,
Future and present, that you're affected,
Mental toil[195] is hard,
Emotional toil is a fear of death,
You can't stay un-infected,
For, life is an infectious and daring game,
Letting you use the powers,
Of all the love and goodness.

---

[195] Hard work

The Unseen Struggles

It's natural to hold emotions,
Not expressing them is your opinion,
Giving up your happiness is always historical,
For people love the giving souls,
It's historic to sacrifice,
And no one knows the wrath,
That you face throughout the life.

Chords of Calm

Peace
Serene
In chaos
Serenity
In the heart and mind,
Music brings solace and love
Finding the real essence
It hits the right chords & emotions
Music brings love and profound essence
The medicine when the soul is medicine-deprived.

Why?

Why is it her fault every time?
She's a woman, treated unimportant.

She must initiate every step, why?
She's the one to cater everyone's dreams.

Why is she hurt & crushed in love?
She cares too much, clinging for love she deserves.

Her ambitions and dreams are crushed, why?
She's immersed in love, forgetting herself.

She's left lonely & unhappy, why?
She's not loved enough in return.

The only question is why it happens?
The answers are still unknown; it's life.

About the Author

Roohi, a published author and holder of a Master's degree in Computer Applications (MCA), navigates the literary world with a multifaceted approach. Her journey into storytelling, content creation, and insightful analysis allows her to not only craft captivating narratives but also offer profound insights into the works of her peers.

With a deep-seated passion for creative expression, Roohi actively engages in the production of evocative stories, lyrical poems, and thought-provoking blog content. Her exploration of diverse themes and emotions through writing reflects her commitment to authentic storytelling and connecting with readers on a profound level.

Roohi's dedication to literature extends beyond creation; she is also recognized as an avid book reviewer, sharing her perspectives and critiques to enrich the reading experience for others. Her role as a content creator and reviewer is complemented by her experience in providing remote content writing services to various organizations, where she applies her literary prowess to produce compelling and impactful written materials.

www.ingramcontent.com/pod-product-compliance
Lightning Source LLC
LaVergne TN
LVHW041943070526
838199LV00051BA/2892